ALSO BY JANET LANESE

::

Grandmothers Are Like Snowflakes

Mothers Are Like Miracles

Sisters Are Like Sunshine

Babies Are Like Blossoms

BY *Proud Grandfathers* AND

Those Who Love AND

Admire Them

COMPILED *by* JANET LANESE

Fireside / PUBLISHED BY SIMON & SCHUSTER

NEW YORK LONDON TORONTO SYDNEY SINGAPORE

GRANDFATHERS ARE LIKE GOLD:

EVERY FAMILY'S TREASURE

::

Anecdotes and Reflections

FIRESIDE
Rockefeller Center
1230 Avenue of the Americas
New York, NY 10020

Permissions Acknowledgments appear on page 128.

Designed by Barbara M. Bachman

Manufactured in the United States of America

1 3 5 7 9 10 8 6 4 2

Library of Congress Cataloging-in-Publication Data
Grandfathers are like gold : every family's treasure : anecdotes and reflections / by proud grandfathers and those who love and admire them ; compiled by Janet Lanese.
p.   cm.
1. Grandfathers—Quotations, maxims, etc. 2. Grandfathers—Quotations. 3. Grandfathers—
Anecdotes. 3. Grandfathers—Poetry. I. Lanese, Janet.
PN6084.G6 G725 2000
306.874'5—dc21
00-026466

ISBN 0-684-86217-4

ACKNOWLEDGMENTS

::

Thanks to Jill Taylor,

my indispensable computer wizard,

who helped me keep my sanity.

Applause to Ruth Weisberg for her valuable input.

All my gratitude to Marcela Landres,

the talented editor at Fireside who kept me

inspired, focused, and organized.

As for Laurie Harper of Sebastian Literary Agency—

she's an author's dream agent!

To 1st Lt. John E. Cantlon of the 509th Squadron,

U.S. Air Force, and pilot of the B-29 *Necessary Evil*.

Not only a hero of World War II but the loving husband of

Cathryn, devoted father of ten children,

proud grandfather of twenty grandkids, and the delighted

great-grandfather of three great-grand babies.

Just one member of America's "greatest generation,"

to whom younger generations owe so much.

CONTENTS

::

HEROES AND WISE MEN

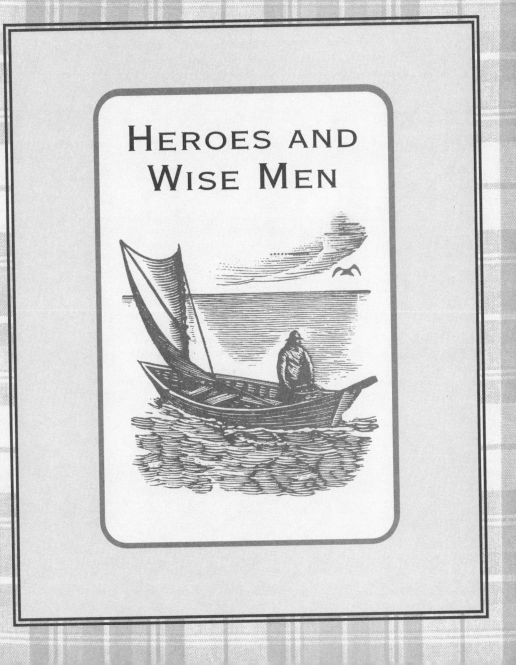

Grandparents, like heroes, are as necessary
to a child's growth as vitamins.

JOYCE ALLSTON

My grandfather was a wonderful role model.
Through him I got to know the gentle side of men.

SARAH LONG

You must teach your children that
the ground beneath their feet is the ashes of
our grandfathers. So they will respect the land,
tell your children that the earth
is rich with the lives of our kin.
Teach your children what we have taught our children,
that the earth is our mother.
Whatever befalls the earth befalls
the sons of the earth.
If men spit upon the ground,
they spit upon themselves.

CHIEF SEATTLE

A Grandfather's Wisdom

The *Wisdom* of making sense of life and appreciating
what I've accomplished.

The *Wisdom* of understanding, and loving my family
without judging.

The *Wisdom* of maintaining integrity regardless of today's
social mores.

The *Wisdom* of accepting circumstances I'm powerless
to change.

The *Wisdom* of preserving my own personal identity,
and high esteem.

The *Wisdom* of adapting to life's cycles and a new
generation.

The *Wisdom* of sharing the pride of roots and traditions.

CHARLES WALTON

A HERO FOR ALL SEASONS

::

Forget about all those overpaid sports stars. A real hero is someone who transcends all generations. John Glenn is such a man.

John Glenn, seventy-seven, grandfather, senator, and astronaut, who was born when men took to the skies in rickety biplanes, is no publicity stunt. What he has been, and is once again, is an authentically American, can-do kind of hero, a profile in courage, who now also ranks as a role model for an aging American society in which seniors won't and don't have to settle for a rocker on the front porch. He is a living example of "You're only as old as you feel."

Glenn's flight on the shuttle Discovery not only tested the limits of space but also powerfully validated what older Americans can do and the contributions they can make. It showed us that it's never too late, and that dreams can be pursued at any age.

Once again the veteran TV newsman Walter Cronkite, eighty-two, covered the event, and Glenn's wife, Annie, and their two children looked on, just as they had in 1962, except this time they were accompanied by Glenn's two teenage grandchildren.

Glenn was forty when he first flew into space thirty-six years ago. Doctors who examined him before this flight said he had the heartbeat and other medical measures of a man still in his forties. That's a tribute to the physical regime Glenn and many seniors—including myself—are following these days and which contributes to vitality and longevity.

Glenn's second launch captivated America as no space mission had for decades. "I don't think grandchildren are ever going to look at their grandparents in the same way again," said Robert Butler, one of the nation's foremost gerontologists, and at seventy-one, director of the International Longevity Center at New York's Mount Sinai Medical Center.

Maybe I'm oversentimental, but I think America owed John Glenn this ride. His courage, his energy, and his indomitable spirit remain an inspiration not just to his generation but to all generations. Godspeed, John Glenn! The best is yet to come.

BERNARD BOGART

Whether a grandfather is a celebrity,
a millionaire, an intellectual, or just
an all-around good guy,
he is a hero to his grandchildren.
No braver knight ever sat at
King Arthur's Round Table than
the man sitting at the head
of the family dining table.

LINDA COLEMAN

Grandfathers are gentle but strong;
to children they are like a port in a storm,
warm and secure.

JOAN BARTLETT

Like a father, a grandfather can preach
a better sermon with his life than his lip.

MEL SCHMIDT

I love to listen to Grandpa's stories.
He's a living history book.

TAMMY, AGE NINE

Remembering Grandfather Chin

::

My paternal grandfather, Grandfather Chin, was the only grandparent I ever met, since my mother's parents died before I was born, and my other grandmother never left Hong Kong. Ah Yeah, which translates into "father of my father," was the kindly and humorous old gentleman I remember.

When I was between six and eight, my grandfather ended up being my surrogate parent because of the long hours my parents worked at their restaurant in New Jersey. I recall that he was of slight build and rather hunched, making his short height even more marked. It wasn't until years later, upon seeing his photo, that I realized he had blue eyes—quite remarkable given the Asiatic genetic trait of brown eyes! I somehow later pieced together that there was some definite mixing somewhere along the generations.

I recall the feel of holding his hand as we walked down the street, watching his intense, mischievous eyes, and his walking me home from the restaurant at night. There is a special trust and comfort that I had with him and a sense that he was old, yet not really. He was part of my young life that became memorable, and perhaps that is in some measure why I have been so committed to intergenerational activity—to assure that continuity and caring and value from one generation to the next.

JENNIE CHIN HANSEN

My grandfather always taught us that
the first step of wisdom is silence,
and the second step is listening.

ARNOLD BETTERMAN

It is the malady of our age that
the young are so busy teaching us that
they have no time left to learn.

ERIC HOFFER

My grandfather once told me
that there were
two kinds of people:
those who do the work and
those who take the credit.
He told me to try to be in the first group;
there was much less competition.

INDIRA GANDHI

When my grandfather speaks,
everyone listens.

JASON, AGE TEN

::

My grandfather grew up with a passionate love for aircraft, but I can't say that as a kid I was fascinated by airplanes. I did not grow up dreaming to be a pilot. At the age of twelve, I had my sights on becoming an electrical engineer. It wasn't until a few years later that I began to think about flying. I admit that my grandfather's role in military aviation helped tip the scale a little, but I never felt pressure stemming from his accomplishments. I love what I'm doing. I love serving our country. What an opportunity. They pay me to go out and challenge myself, fly state-of-the-art equipment, and have a good time.

The world today is a lot scarier than when my grandfather dropped the atomic bomb on Hiroshima. We knew who our enemies were. Today, anyone could be our enemy. We don't know who's going to want to take us on next. When I entered the Air Force Academy, Mother Russia was our enemy. It's a much more uncertain world out there.

As for my grandfather, it's an honor to have his name.

PAUL TIBBETS IV

We all know grandparents whose values transcend passing fads and pressures, and who possess the wisdom of distilled pain and joy.

JIMMY CARTER

Grandfathers are for telling you what it used to be like, but not too much.

CHARLES SHEDD

*My grandpa reads his Bible all the time.
I wonder if he's cramming for his finals.*

LAURIE, AGE NINE

*Grandfathers impart information,
ethics, and values
that children learn nowhere else.*

ARTHUR KORNHABER

WHERE HAVE YOU GONE, JOE DIMAGGIO?

Are our grandfathers' heroes our heroes?

::

Only once in a blue moon, an individual makes such an impact on our society that his name is passed down through generations. Joe DiMaggio was such a man. He will live forever in the hearts and minds of baseball fans, young and old alike.

They called him Jolting Joe and the Yankee Clipper, and when Joe DiMaggio died in 1999 at eighty-four, a style and an era ended.

New York newspaper columnist Jimmy Breslin once wrote, "Baseball isn't statistics; it's Joe DiMaggio rounding second base."

He was a larger-than-life celebrity. Hemingway fictionalized him, Simon and Garfunkel immortalized him, Marilyn Monroe romanticized him, Mr. Coffee commercialized him, and a fifty-six-game hitting streak made him a national sports treasure. The record endures as the last great sports record still to be broken. In 1955, Joe was inducted into baseball's Hall of Fame.

While Joe played thirteen seasons with the New York Yankees, his heroics were not limited to baseball. He was involved in many philanthropic causes. A modest and private man, he preferred to keep a low profile, and did his best work anonymously. Many people don't know that in 1992, he donated his name and time to raise money for a children's wing of Memorial Regional Hospital in southern Florida. The result is a state-of-the-art, 150-bed facility. True to Joe's philosophy, no child is denied treatment because of inability to pay.

Joe, a grandfather of two and a great-grandfather of four, was really involved and a frequent visitor at the hospital. You could tell how much he loved kids by the way he interacted with the young patients. Several years ago, my grandfather and I were visiting my brother, who was a patient, and had the privilege of shaking the legend's hand and talking a "little" baseball. My grandfather bragged about the encounter with his sports idol until the day he died, and my brother, who is now a first baseman for his high school team, will always remember the man who was his inspiration and role model.

After DiMaggio's death, former Mayor Ed Koch summed up Joe's life perfectly:

"He represented the best in America," Koch said. "It was his character, his generosity, his sensitivity. He was someone who set a standard every father in the world would want his children to follow."

JIM THURSTON

As a grandfather,
I'm entitled to a few words
of sage advice to the young:
I would spend more time
with my children.

JOHN HUSTON

One of the odd things about ancestors,
even if they are no older than grandfathers,
is that we can scarcely help feeling that,
compared to them, we are degenerate.

ROBERT LYND

Each generation imagines itself to be
more intelligent than the one
that went before it,
and wiser than the one that comes after it.

GEORGE ORWELL

My Grandfather's Story

::

The first time I heard my grandfather's full story was when I decided to interview him for a genealogy project in seventh grade. I still remember his tears when he told me that when the Nazis took him away from home, he realized that he would never see his parents again. His courage and determination astounded me when I heard how he managed to smuggle food into the Lodz ghetto for his family. Leib, his Polish name, meaning lion, is truly a fitting name. In October 1940, my grandfather was taken to a labor camp along with two hundred other people from Lodz. There he was reduced to eating grass for six months, and every day of survival was an interminable struggle.

In August 1943, my grandfather arrived in Auschwitz-Birkenau. This was the first time he had seen a German soldier. Previously he had seen Polish, Ukrainian, and Estonian soldiers. It was also the first time he realized that the Jews were being mass-exterminated. He got the number 143248 tattooed on his arm, and it can still be seen to this day.

After traveling to various other camps, my grandfather

stopped at Ohrdruf. There the seemingly never-ending torture came to an end. My grandfather mustered up his last vestiges of strength and escaped the death march from which few others returned. Upon returning to the camp, my grandfather spied a foreign army, the American army. From there my grandfather's story only got better.

With the help of two wonderful friends, Ben Kaplan and Al Schwartz, my grandfather eventually found himself in America. In the land of opportunity, he landed a job in the K. Wolens department stores and spent the next thirty-one years with this company. He married Shirley, my wonderful grandmother, and had four daughters. Today, my grandparents have ten loving grandchildren, me being one of them. In 1981, my grandfather found Shmuel Laufer and Shmuel Tusk alive in Israel. He finally discovered that he was not the only survivor of his big family; he was no longer alone in the world.

Of all the emotions conjured up by my grandfather's story, one stands out the most. Here I am sitting in a beautiful house, free from oppression, free from hunger, free from anything that could restrict my freedom, yet only fifty years ago, six million Jews experienced exactly the opposite. They went through a hell which I cannot even fathom. I was filled with feelings of guilt, horror, and sadness, yet at the same time I was incredibly happy. I marveled at the miraculous change that my grandfather and the Jews as a whole underwent. Israel, a dream which had gone unfulfilled for 2,000 years, has been established. The Holocaust survivors have regenerated the Jewish nation by creating successful families and new communities. We are free to practice our religion and customs wherever we wish. It is truly a miracle, which G-d willing, will bring to an end two thousand years of suffering.

GILAD EVRONY

"Everyone should be a grandparent
before they're a parent."
I don't know who first penned this
genetically impossible advice;
they're right.
We grandparents have much better hindsight
than foresight.

MIKE BELLAH

If a grandfather hasn't learned
something from experience, he can always
consult a grandchild.

AL GOLDSMITH

It's in the Genes

Every grandfather believes in heredity
until his grandchildren start
making fools of themselves.

SIMON SCHWARTZ

I have to admit my two grandchildren
rarely misquote me. In fact, they have
quite a knack for repeating word for word
some remark I shouldn't have made
in the first place.

LYLE GOLDBERG

You've got to do your own growing,
no matter how tall your grandfather was.

IRISH PROVERB

The five most important questions
any small grandchild asks are
  1. Why?
  2. Why?
  3. Why?
  4. Why?
  5. Why?

THOMAS KLINE

A grandfather is a man who
used to sit up waiting for his
teenage children to come home.
Now he sits up with his middle-age children
waiting for their teenage children to come home.

ROBERT CROSS

I'm not the least bit worried what and how
much my teenage grandkids know.
But it sure makes me nervous wondering
how they found out.

MELVIN LEVITZ

To my grandson, seventeen,
walking distance is that between
the garage and the telephone.

JON SCHMIDT

A grandfather is a man
who can't understand how
his idiot son has such brilliant children.

MILTON BERLE

Normally I don't believe in miracles, but
something happened when I was about seven years old
I still can't explain. I was on the front porch
with Grandpa, about to eat my Twinkies,
when Grandpa started grabbing his chest and
saying he was having a heart attack.
I ran to get Mom, but when I got back,
Grandpa was okay. "An angel helped me," he said.
"Also, he ate your Twinkies."

JACK HANDY

When I started to tell my nine-year-old grandson
the facts of life, a bored look came over his face,
and he said, "Grandpa, before you go into any great detail,
just how many are there?"

RON JORY

My son is in graduate school, and my grandson is in
kindergarten. Most days you can hardly tell the difference.

JAMES PIERCE

I wish Mom and Dad would take lessons
from Grandpa on parenting.

SALLY, AGE EIGHT

DISGUSTED GRANDFATHER:
"Why in heaven's name did you fall in the mud puddle
with your dress on?"

FIVE-YEAR-OLD GRANDDAUGHTER:
"What else could I do? There wasn't time to take it off!"

JOHN PHILLIPS

Grandchildren: expensive, time-consuming,
patience-taxing additions to any family, but the
sacrifices they require are insignificant compared
to the love we feel in return.

CHAD WALTERS

Heredity: Something you believe in when your grandson
graduates from Stanford, Magna Cum Laude, with a Ph.D.

JAMES LONG

What makes a boy more brilliant than
being a grandson?

TOM BERG

I wonder if my grandpa was ever a father.

STEPHANIE, AGE FIVE

Believe it or not,
youngsters don't know everything.
My grandson can't understand why
a man kisses a girl's neck just
because she has a good pair of legs.

NEIL BLANKENSHIP

I knew my teenage grandson was
really growing up
when he stopped complaining about
feeling sick
watching movie love scenes.

TODD ELWOOD

Like sale merchandise that is marked "as is,"
grandchildren need to be accepted with
whatever imperfections they may have.
This has nothing to do with coddling,
but rather with offering a center of strength for
children who may not find it anywhere else.

LILLIAN CARSON

Poo Poo, Itsy Bitsy, Cutesy Coo
To this babble baby listens
By the hour, day and week
And yet the grandpa wonders
Will she ever learn to speak?

ROGER MULLENS

*Grandchildren are wonderful, but nothing
is more embarrassing than having to beg
your ten-year-old granddaughter to
help you program your new computer.*

TED KRAUSE

*Feel the dignity of a child. Do not feel
superior to him, for you are not.*

ROBERT HENRI

*When I was a youngster,
I used to have to kneel and pray for long periods with
my grandfather, who prayed aloud in
an unintelligible mutter. One day I finally found the
courage to tell him that I couldn't understand a word
of his prayers. My grandfather slowly lifted up his head
and looked at me with disdain.
"I wasn't speaking to you," he retorted.*

BILL COSBY

GREAT-GRANDPA:
"Junior, can you think of anything worse than being old and bent?"

COLLEGE STUDENT:
"Yes, Gramps, being young and broke."

STEVEN LEDERMAN

I must admit that I was really disappointed my grandson didn't inherit his father's athletic ability. That was before he scored 1500 on his SAT test.

RICHARD SUMMERFIELD

Sara, age nine, said to her grandma, "Wow, did Grandpa take me for a joy ride in his Jeep! We passed two morons, three jackasses, four stupids, and I can't count how many crazies!"

MANUEL SANCHEZ

*Feeding your grandbaby strained carrots is
one sure way to find out how badly your
new golf shirt stains.*

RICHARD BLASS

PROUD GRANDFATHER:

*"My grandson is only two, and has been walking since
he was eight months old."*

UNIMPRESSED FRIEND:

"Poor little guy, he must be pooped!"

MELVIN SANDERS

My grandpa told me
he was a soldier in the Korean War.
I think that was about the time
Lincoln was shot.

AMY, AGE NINE

Warren, age eight, was asked by his grandfather,
"What's the first thing you notice about a girl?"
"Well, that all depends on which direction she's facing."

MILTON BERLE

My grandfather's hair used to be parted.
Now it's departed.

SALLY, AGE TWELVE

Young boy showing his grandparent's photo album
to a school chum:
"Now you know why I threw all my
comic books away when I found this!"

PETE SMALL

My grandkids still can't figure out how I managed to get through childhood without a giant-screen color TV, a DVD player, and a laptop computer.

SAM ALLISON

I have two beautiful grandchildren, but just to be on the safe side, I'm trying to convince my son and daughter-in-law to have another. That way if one turns out to be a genius, the other two can help support him.

MEL BRUNER

A teenager who learns from his grandfather how much gasoline a dollar used to buy must feel pretty discouraged.

PHIL SCOTT

I keep asking my grandpa why I only get to go to the beach this summer, while Casey's grandpa keeps promising to send him to the moon.

BOBBY, AGE SIX

GREAT-GRANDSON:

"To what do you attribute your old age, Gramps?"

GREAT-GRANDFATHER:

"Well, Junior, it's very simple. I was born a long time ago."

STAN MACKEY

I love my grandpa's bald head.
It's so neat.

JODY, AGE EIGHT

Greatness of name in the father
ofttimes overwhelms the son;
they stand too near one another.
The shadow kills the growth so much,
that we see the grandchild come more and
oftener to be heir to the first.

SAMUEL JOHNSON

I keep telling my grandchildren,
they're going to have a hard time
paying for the good times
I never had.

JEFFREY SANDS

TIRED MOTHER RETURNING HOME FROM WORK:
  "I hope my little darling has been as good as gold all day."

EXHAUSTED GRANDFATHER BABYSITTING:
  "No, dear, I'm afraid he went off the gold standard about an hour after you left."

JESSE BLANKENSHIP

The older my grandpa gets, the farther he had to walk to school.

HEATHER, AGE FIFTEEN

Never say (to young people) "that was before your time," because the last full moon was before their time.

BILL COSBY

My grandfather is not old, he's just an obsolete boy.

LAURIE, AGE SIXTEEN

Grandma was sure lucky when
she snagged Grandpa.
He's lived such an exciting life.
He is the only person I know
who's met three dead presidents.

RYAN, AGE TEN

It was hard to let go,
but I finally made the decision to
let my sixteen-year-old grandson shift for himself.
I feel it's better he do it now,
while he still knows everything.

LINCOLN MORROW

When I was voted the best artist
in the fourth grade, Grandpa took a lot of the credit.
He claims I inherited
my talent from his side of the family.

JENNY, AGE NINE

Nothing you do for children is ever wasted.
They seem not to notice us hovering, averting our eyes,
and they seldom offer thanks; but what we
do for them is never wasted.

GARRISON KEILLOR

A Kid's
Best Friend

*It is one of nature's ways that
we often feel closer to
distant generations than to
the generations immediately preceding us.*

IGOR STRAVINSKY

*The most precious thing I can
give to my grandkids
is not my money, but my time.*

FRANK BROWN

*Grandparents help kids understand and settle into a world
which can be pretty confusing to newcomers.*

CHARLES SLAYBAUGH

THE BOWL OF MILK

::

The swaying trees cast mobile shadows on the empty driveway, the pale moon just a glimpse of silver between their leaves. The dark of night envelops me, as it creeps up to where I am sitting, alone on a wooden step leading up to the porch. In my hands is a bowl of milk for the stray cats.

The milk glimmers like a mirror, and all of a sudden, I am reminded of the time at the lake, when Grandpa was alive. We sat side by side, fishing rods bobbing in the flowing water.

I don't remember if we caught any fish that day, but I clearly remember looking into the water and seeing our reflection. Together we looked content, at peace.

Grandpa helped Janie and me build a treehouse near the lake. We built it high above the ground and painted it green in hopes that it would be camouflaged by the leaves and remain our secret.

It was a beautiful treehouse. Janie and I spent a lot of our childhood up there. Grandpa would sometimes come up and tell us wonderful stories of the farm he grew up on and how he had to wake up early in the morning to feed the chickens before the long walk to school. There was more to the stories than that. There was always a magical touch to them. Grandpa was known for his magical touch. It shined in his eyes, which were deep blue, childlike, with the oldest of age-old wisdom. Grandpa told us that the farm came alive in the mornings. The animals talked, the grass and wheat danced, and the breeze sang to him.

It was Grandpa who comforted me when Janie went off to college. I missed her so much. To take my mind off of it, Grandpa took me outside to feed the stray cats that roamed the area. We placed a bowl of milk on the grass before us, sat on the step, and waited. Soon, mangy cats of all different breeds came to feed. Their eyes darted nervously as they lapped up the milk. In the twilight, their eyes seemed to have a magic like Grandpa's in them.

I now place a bowl of milk in the grass, just like Grandpa did, and wait for the stray cats. It's amazing how many memories come alive with a bowl of milk.

MARIE HOY, FIFTEEN,
MISSISSAUGA, ONTARIO, CANADA

GRANDMA? GRANDPA?

::

The phrase "baby boomer grandparents" is quite the oxymoron. Being a simple soul, I refuse to acknowledge such a contradictory concept, preferring to see the world as no more complicated than the abstractions one might encounter in, say, *Dick and Jane*—my favorite book.

But adopting the guise of "objective reporter" I must force myself to recognize other people's skewed notions of reality. As in point, an author recently contacted me and informed "yours truly" that there are people my age who are now grandparents. . . .

Ha! Prove it to me! I want DNA tests!

It seems he is involved in a project with another writer preparing a guide for baby boomers on grandparenting.

Now . . . where could the market be for this? Sounds like cheesy genre writing to me—undoubtedly slapped under the heading of Science Fiction or Paranormal Phenomena. I might even stick it in the Humor section (that's because I know this knockout blonde around my age who claims to be a grandmother—and when she talks about it I just laugh in her face).

I plan on relating to this author an account of how I was abducted by space aliens who looked like grandchildren (beamed up to their flying saucer, I was forced to bounce them on my knee and feed them candy). It's a much more believable story.

CHUCK NYREN

When grandparents enter the door,
discipline flies out the window.

OGDEN NASH

When Grandpa gave me that ten dollars and
asked me to go to the store and
get some groceries for him, I knew I had a choice:
I could go buy candy and gumballs for me
and friends, or I could buy model airplanes.

JACK HANDY

The quickest way to be convinced that
spanking and child abuse are
synonymous is to become a grandfather.

GERALD FROST

When you crave something sweet or expensive,
it's best to call your grandparents.

ROGER, AGE ELEVEN

The skin any grandkid loves to touch:
his grandfather's old pigskin wallet.

CALVIN SMITH

A grandpa is a nice man who
comes to your house,
spoils you rotten, and
then kisses you
on the cheek and goes home.

SAMANTHA, AGE SIX

What the average grandpa
would really like to say
to his grandson at the dinner table is,
"Go ahead and eat my broccoli, Junior!"

PHILIP MYER

THAT'S WHAT GRANDFATHERS ARE FOR

Sometimes your father tells you,
"You're making such a mess!"
Sometimes your mother says to you,
"You're wrinkling up my dress!"

Sometimes your teacher scolds you:
"You're making too much noise!"
Sometimes your best friend tells you,
"Now don'cha touch my toys!"

You look so sad, and whisper,
"No one loves me anymore."
"I always do!" I tell you—
"That's what grandfathers are for!"

ARLENE S. USLANDER

*Just ask any kid. A grandfather can keep
a secret better than the CIA.*

FRANK LOWELL

You know why grandfathers make the best babysitters?

Because they don't raid the refrigerator.

JIM COLE

*Grandparents somehow sprinkle
a sense of stardust
over grandchildren.*

ALEX HALEY

*I can always tell when my grandfather enters a room.
It's that delicious aftershave lotion he wears.*

JENNY, AGE FOURTEEN

THE HAPPY LITTLE TRAVELER

He always likes to travel
and it fills me full of pride,
when I'm driving down the highway
with my grandson at my side.

He's a happy little fellow
with the sweetest little smiles,
and we have a joyful visit,
as we click away the miles!

RALPH REITENOUR

MY GRANDPA'S COWS

My grandpa was a funny man,
full of rhyme and wit.
He told me lots of stories
that didn't seem to fit.

He took me driving in the hills.
We talked about the cow
whose legs are short on the uphill side
to keep from falling down.

He said the white cows give plain milk,
but if you like it flavored,
the brown cow serves up chocolate milk,
the best you've ever savored.

If buttermilk is what you like,
you need to find a black cow.
I asked if spotted ones gave cheese,
"You've got that right, and how!"

I listened to his stories.
And laughed till I was blue.
I hadn't the heart to tell him
I knew that they weren't true.

GINI SUNNERGREN

There are fathers who do not love their children;
there is no grandfather who
does not adore his grandson.

VICTOR HUGO

Grandfathers don't count on parents or fairy godmothers
to insure that their grandkids' lives are happy.
They do everything in their power to make them that way.

CONRAD MCCOY

Why does it seem unusual for grandfathers
to introduce kids to sports?
To our generation sports are the
toy department of human life.

SYDNEY LONG

GRAMPS

They're kind, sharing and happy. They give you hugs and do their best to play with you. They call you pet names and make jokes about you, but they're not mean jokes. They try with all their patience to hang around you. Even if you're young they treat you equally.

JUAN PABLO ARDILO, AGE ELEVEN,
SAN JOSÉ, COSTA RICA

My grandpa is so handsome and lovable that
I only wish I was old enough to marry him.
But I guess Grandma would get jealous.
You know how older women are about us younger ones.

SARAH, AGE SEVEN

Because grandparents are usually free to love
and guide and befriend the young without
having to take daily responsibility for them,
they can often reach out past pride
and fear of failure and close the
space between generations.

JIMMY CARTER

It's not a myth, but a fact, that only a grandpa
can cast a line into a stream, and snag
the biggest trout a grandkid's ever seen.

MARK MCCOY

What a great guy my grandpa is!
Every time we go fishing,
he always makes sure we catch our limit,
even if it takes dropping by
Tony's Fish Market to do it.

MARK, AGE TEN

To My Grandfather

Did I ever say "thank you"
for the time you spent with me
while I was growing up?

For loving me unconditionally and
believing in me?

I can only hope I can teach my
grandchildren what you taught me.

FRIEDA MCREYNOLDS

I can cry and laugh with my grandkids like
I never did with my own kids.
Becoming a grandfather
has made me grow up.

DADDY WELLS

I know my grandpa loves me.
He wears a sweatshirt with my name on it.

GRETCHEN, AGE FIVE

A baby has a way of making a man
out of his father, and a boy out of his grandfather.

ANGIE PAPADAKIS

With a grandfather, kids don't have to perform,
as they must for their parents, peers, and teachers.
We love and accept them just as they are.

MARIO THONI

Who but a grandfather can—

- *Make everything OK with a big bear hug.*
- *Always find change for an ice-cream cone.*
- *Fix any broken toy better than new.*
- *Know the best picnic and fishing spots.*
- *Pop tastier popcorn than a movie theater.*
- *Imitate the voices of all the cartoon characters.*
- *Tell the scariest ghost stories.*
- *Plan the greatest vacations.*
- *Talk parents into or out of anything.*

TERRI MARQUEZ

I don't think grandpas get enough pats on the back.

SUSIE, AGE EIGHT

When my son had the temerity to have a child,
I hung a sign in my office, "The first one to call me
Grandpa gets his ass fired." Not all of us think grandkids
are the greatest—but that was before I met mine.

TONY BARRETT

*One of the most powerful handclasps
is that of a new grandbaby around
the finger of a grandfather.*

JOY HARGROVE

*Grandpa . . . was ever ready to cheer and
help me, ever sure that I was
a remarkable specimen.
He was a dear old man who
asked little from life
and got less.*

MILES FRANKLIN

*Grandchildren want to know everything
about grandfathers:*

What were we like as children?

How did we feel growing up in our families?

What was our neighborhood like?

How did we do in school?

Who were our friends?

What were our hobbies?

What were our dreams?

What were our fears?

The turning points in our lives?

The experiences that shaped us as people?

And, of course, how did we meet the grandmothers
    we married?

Stories about grandfathers are exciting to grandchildren,
    and will live on for generations to come.

ARNOLD PATTON

An Understanding Soul

::

In my experience, there is always a special person who stands out and treats you like royalty. In my case it was my grandpa.

He was the nicest person in the world to me. He never lost his temper, even when my grandma lost hers and threw dishes on the floor. He would just sit there and wait until she was done, and then talk with her calmly.

He had to deal with many things in his lifetime. In fact, I am quite surprised that he could be so understanding all those years. Between my mother being extremely ill, my father abusing her, and raising me, my grandpa still had enough love and patience to help everyone. To tell the truth, he only had one fault; he was always late, no matter what.

Unfortunately, he died when I was five years old. I truly do miss him, his jokes, the ice cream bars he would buy after dinner, even his lateness.

Heather Carollo, age fifteen,
Makakilo, Hawaii

My grandpa taught me to play checkers.
He read stories to me, and he helped me build
my first model. He showed me how to reach out
with my bat, and hit a curve ball.
He always rooted for my team.

JOAN FASSLER

Being grandparents sufficiently removes us from
the responsibilities so that we can be friends—
really good friends.

ALAN FROME

The best games between children and grandfathers are
timeless, and there seems to be nothing better to bridge the
generation gap than play.

VINCENT MACKENZIE

Every generation revolts against its fathers and
makes friends with its grandfathers.

LEWIS MUMFORD

GRANDPARENTS ARE LIKE THAT . . .

::

Grandmothers, it seems, have special places in the hearts of their grandchildren and will forever maintain those places simply by being typical grandmas. Not to be outdone, grandfathers have never taken a back seat in their roles in the lives of their grandchildren.

Grandfathers let the dog sit on the car upholstery and lick from your ice-cream cone.

Grandfathers go for walks, go fishing, and explain caterpillars.

Grandfathers sit in wet sand, allowing castles to be built in their laps.

Grandfathers do things no other segment of humans do. For instance, they go to a bird's funeral.

Grandfathers explain where kittens go when they die and what happens to the sun at night.

Grandfathers call you things like "Pumpkin" and "Bunny Rabbit," and somehow it's all right.

Grandfathers don't begin sentences with "I'm really busy now," and they don't object to walking through the toy department.

Grandfathers determinedly race across the grass, holding tightly to the string of a sky-soaring kite long after their grandchildren have wandered away bored.

Grandfathers sit in the shallow end of the pool.

Grandfathers don't cringe when handed a dozen little books at story time.

It has been said that grandchildren are God's compensation for growing old. Perhaps it should also be said that grandfathers are gifts of love, understanding, and knowledge far beyond the vision of youth.

CAROL KAPEL COX

LIFE IN PRIME TIME

When I was a father, my kids disagreed with
about 99 percent of my opinions.
Now that I'm a grandfather,
anything I say is terrific.

PETER MANSFIELD

Nothing makes you feel older than the knowledge that
your grandchildren are studying in history class
what you studied in current events.

SAL MILLS

Do you realize how lonely it is for a grandfather to
grow old alone? Why, my wife hasn't had a birthday
in five years!

KEN LARSON

Experience is what enables you to recognize
a mistake when you make it again.

EARL WILSON

FIVE FAMOUS LAST WORDS FOR MIDLIFERS

- *My teenager would never do that.*

- *Old dogs can't learn new tricks.*

- *Don't worry, my knee can handle it.*

- *I'll have just one more piece of this cheesecake.*

- *So how hard can it be to raise a grandchild?*

MIKE BELLAH

"Don't worry about senility,"
my grandfather used to say.
"When it hits you, you won't know it."

BILL COSBY

My grandma and grandpa still act like kids.
They have a sign on their door that says,
"Do not disturb, grandparents at play."

MATT, AGE TEN

By the time a man reaches
the age of a grandfather,
he usually has given up physically abusive sports
such as football and basketball and
replaced them with mentally abusive games
such as golf and poker.

RICK GRADY

It's hard to know when one generation ends
and the next one begins.
But it's somewhere around
nine o'clock at night.

CHARLES RUFFING

Of course my grandfather doesn't
date women his own age!
There aren't any.

ROBERTA, AGE THIRTEEN

Today's "cool" grandfathers have switched from:

Leisure suits to designer jeans

Hush Puppies to Nikes

Toupees to transplants

Gas guzzlers to sporty compacts

Couch potatoes to power walkers

Retirement to entrepreneuring

Martinis to Chardonnay

Cha cha to line dancing

Mobile homes to condos

Bifocals to contact lenses

TV dinners to Healthy Gourmet

Arizona Winnebagos to European elderhostels

PETE SMALLEY

*Many grandfathers discover that to be sixty
is a lot less complex and stressful than to be thirty.*

NICHOLAS WEST

*My grandpa looks young,
but I figure his age has to be
somewhere between Mickey Mouse's
and Santa Claus's.*

TIMMY, AGE SEVEN

*A grandfather knows
he's getting old when he
starts letting his granddaughter
pick out his neckties.*

SIMON LEVINE

*By the time a grandfather can
afford to lose a golf ball, he can't hit it that far.*

SY BERG

My grandmother and grandfather
are having trouble with their ages.
He refuses to act his, and she refuses to tell hers.

MELODY, AGE SIXTEEN

YOUTH!
Stay close to the young and a little rubs off.

ALAN JAY LERNER

When dealing with small children,
many a grandfather has given in
because he's given out.

TOM FOSTER

A married daughter with children
puts you in danger
of being catalogued as a first edition.

WARWICK DEEPING

I asked my grandfather, who has been married
for over fifty years, his secret for longevity.

"That's easy," he said.
"It's all about outlasting your opponent."

LINDA BROWN

Now that Grandpa is retired, Grandma says
he's only useful for two things:
lawn care and car maintenance.

SARA, AGE EIGHT

Ours seems to be the only nation on earth that asks
its teenagers what to do about world affairs,
and tells its golden-agers to go out and play.

JULIAN GROW

I don't mind being a grandfather, except that it means
I have to sleep with a grandmother.

MILTON BERLE

HAIRSTYLIST:
  "What kind of haircut do you want, little girl?"

LITTLE GIRL:
  "The same kind as my grandpa gets, bangs with a hole
  on top of my head."

JOHN STEELE

*I think my grandpa is either losing it
or going through his second childhood.
He just asked my orthodontist
to put braces on his false teeth.*

ALY, AGE TWELVE

*Definition of a baby boomer grandpa:
A man who hires a handyman and gardener to do
his weekend chores while he is out coaching
his granddaughter's soccer team.*

SAM KLINK

When I first heard the news
from my daughter that
I was about to be a grandfather,
it sort of made me feel like an old fogey.
But when I read that the
ultra-stud Pierce Brosnan's
stepdaughter Charlotte was also expecting,
I said to myself, Well, hell, what's good enough
for James Bond is good enough for me!
I'm going to follow his lead as
the World's Sexiest Grandpa.

STUART ANDERSON

Little Mark was looking through his grandparents' photo album.

"Who's that young guy with all the muscles lying on the beach with you, Grandma?"

"Why, that's your grandpa, sweetie."

"You have to be kidding. That's my grandpa? Then who's that old pot-bellied geezer living with you now?"

BOB SELLERS

If you see a middle-aged friend, who looks pale and haggard and complains about being broke, he's probably just spent a week's vacation with his teenage grandchildren.

JIM SWANSON

My grandpa keeps saying he's
a "baby boomer."
Is that some kind of
supercharged babysitter?

TIMMY, AGE SIX

Definition of a senior power walker:
A grandfather with two cars—
one driven by his wife,
the other driven by his teenage grandchild.

ADOLPH SMITH

My grandson is fifteen and
I'm in my late fifties.
You can imagine how he took it
when this old man beat his time
in the San Francisco, Bay to Breakers.
I bet he starts training earlier next year.

GEORGE KELBY

GRANDSON:
  "Grandpa, why don't you get a hearing aid?"

GRANDFATHER:
  "Don't need it. I hear more now than I can understand."

MILTON BERLE

Two great-grandfathers shooting the bull:

"You're an old man!"
"I'm old? When you were young,
the Dead Sea was only sick."

MILTON BERLE

My grandpa doesn't work anymore.
He goes to his office every day,
and then once in a while runs an errand
on his way home.

SANDY, AGE SEVEN

My grandkids won't believe this
is my own hair, but it is.
I paid good money for it.

KELSEY BROWN

My grandpa says I look just like him.
But I can't figure how he got that idea—
I don't have a mustache,
a double chin, or a pot belly.

JASON, AGE TEN

When does a man stop hiding his age?
When he brings out his wallet to
show pictures of his grandchildren.

BILL COX

A Grand Tradition

Grandfathers are made in heaven,
born fully formed with the birth
of their first grandchild.

RUTH GOODE

The nicest thing I can think about
having grandchildren
is that you're not too busy supporting
them to enjoy them.

BILL MITCHELL

A child is born, and for twenty years makes
so much noise we think we'll go mad, and then
he departs leaving the home so silent that we think
we'll never get over the loneliness.
But if we're lucky, the situation is remedied
when a grandbaby is born,
and the cycle repeats itself.

BOB MILLER

GRAMPS OR GRANDPA, THE ROLE IS REALLY JUST GRAND

::

Christian Aaron, on the night before you were born, a bone-china moon, radiant with a halo of haze, drew your mother to the window. Superstition would have me believe that the moon whispered your name then, telling you it was time.

I could be wrong. The whispering might have been the toppings on the pizza she had eaten a few hours earlier.

You waited awhile before setting up the ruckus that heralded your birth, Thursday at twelve minutes past noon on the twelfth day of the twelfth month of the year.

I was three cups of coffee into the waning pages of Carrie Young's *The Wedding Dress* when your grinning father, Jim, popped into the maternity waiting room to announce your arrival.

"What's it gonna be?" son Aaron asked, draping an arm over my shoulder. "Grandpa? Gramps? Grandfather?"

For nine months I have been listening to the question: "How does it make you feel that you're going to be a grandfather?"

Just fine, Christian Aaron. Just fine.

Grandparents are pretty good teachers about the things that matter in life.

There is, of course, a reason for that.

As people grow older, they often rediscover the commonplace wonders of the physical world around them; first snow and dogwood blossoms, the smell of rain on the wind, the frolic sculpture of Orion on a clear night.

You lose sight of those things for a while when, ironically, you are consumed with rearing your own children, making ends meet, keeping up appearances.

They come back to you, though, when fate gives you a grandchild at just the right time.

Not coincidentally, it is the same time you begin to realize the petty folly, shallowness, and predictability of much of what you once thought mattered.

If I can teach you anything about being humane and compassionate, I will be doing more than I ever could have hoped.

But just now, Christian Aaron, I'm not thinking about all that. I'm trying to remember which box in the basement

Curious George is hiding in, and the lyrics to the third verse of "Hobo's Lullaby."

And all I heard when your mother held you up for me to see was, "How come you're crying, Dad?"

MIKE HARDEN

*From the days of the first grandfather,
everyone has remembered
a golden age behind him.*

JAMES RUSSELL LOWELL

*A great-grandfather is a man who
remembers when
you needed help to carry
ten dollars' worth of groceries.*

BRENT COLLIER

I've never had a burning desire
to be a grandfather,
but now I feel it's one of
life's greater pleasures—
feeling those little hands
patting my face is pure ecstasy.

WALTER CRONKITE

THE GRANDPARENT NAME GAME

::

Whatever happened to *Bubbe* and *Zayda?* No, not their whereabouts. Their names! Of course, you know where—and how—they are: They're doing just fine and probably living in Florida. As today's baby boomers look forward to grandparenthood (if they haven't already reached that milestone), will they want their grandchildren to use the same Old World names for them that they once used to address their own grandparents?

Bubbe and *zayda* are the Yiddish words for grandmother and grandfather. Sadly, not only is the aging generation of people who originally spoke this colorful and descriptive mother tongue dying off, but so is the language itself.

So what are today's children calling their modern-day grandparents? There are still many bubbes and zaydas, and even more grandmoms and grandpops, but leave it to those creative grandchildren to come up with their own unique names.

Craig Snider, son of Philadelphia Flyers ice hockey team owner Ed Snider, called Sol, his grandfather, Huppi. Apparently, when the oldest grandchild was a toddler, Sol would play with him by bouncing him on his knee. When he wanted to bounce some more, he'd say to his grandfather, "Up high, up high." Only he pronounced it Huppi. The name stuck, and all his other grandchildren called him that. He even had a license plate that said Huppi.

Never mind that Marty Kreithen is a prominent Philadelphia attorney and a flourishing artist who has had his paintings exhibited at area art galleries. To his grandchildren and extended family, he's simply Deet. "When my grandchildren were born, I'd hold them in my arms, dance around, and sing 'deet deet deet' to them. Now all six grandchildren and even my son-in-law call me Deet."

Fortunately there are certain Yiddish words (e.g., *shlep* and *kvetch*) that have already become part of the general vernacular. *Bubbe* and *zayda* may also make a similar leap into the mainstream. And even though grandparents may have changed their looks and lifestyles from one generation to the next, these Old World terms of endearment are still sacrosanct.

RUTH WEISBERG

Who but a great-grandfather
remembers the good old days
when inflation was just
something you did to the kids' balloons
on the Fourth of July?

FRANK GRAHAM

Who but a grandchild can—

- *Teach you to act like a kid again.*
- *Supply you with endless hugs and kisses.*
- *Make every holiday more meaningful.*
- *Help you shape up, mentally, and physically.*
- *Let you in on all the family secrets.*
- *Test your patience and endurance.*
- *Keep you up on the latest clothing and music fads.*
- *Give you a second chance at parenting.*
- *Share the excitement of the moment.*
- *Add a new branch to the family tree.*

FRANK ALCORN

The grandfathering principle is
to pretend not to notice anything children
do when parents are present,
and when they're not, to intervene only to
preserve life, limb, and sanity.

RICHARD FRISBIE

My granddad was a captain in the Marines and
was awarded the silver star, and a purple heart.
But he never thinks of himself as a brave war hero.

"Every American who served in Vietnam
was a hero," he tells us.
"Thousands of men, and many women,
paid the ultimate price for
their devotion to a country of people who
were largely opposed to this war, and
spat on the image of 'the military.'
Thank God I have lived long enough to see
a change of heart. Our veterans are finally starting
to get the credit they deserve.
Unfortunately, it is too late for too many.
I can only pray that my grandchildren
and great-grandchildren will be
spared the same fate."

TOM SANDERS, SIXTEEN

Grandbabies are better than babies.
You can tote them around the church,
collecting compliments,
whereas it would be unseemly if
you were merely the father.

OREN ARNOLD

In spite of all their mess'n
Grandkids are a bless'n.

ANONYMOUS GRANDFATHER

SHORT TAKES

::

My official U.S. government Medicare card arrived in the mail last month with a note that I could start using it April 1, which must be the government's idea of subtle humor. I have since been trying to figure out the other benefits of being 65. Sure, getting there, but being a grandfather tops that.

Without any practice, I am doing the grandfather thing well. That is mostly my 21-month-old granddaughter Mira's doing. Mira's vocabulary is small, but she expresses love like a master. All I have to do is sit around looking pleasant and occasionally read a book aloud. She calls me Papa.

She shouts, "Oh boy, Papa!" when she hears I'm on the phone. She offers, unasked, a precious, soggy Froot Loop. She lets me help with the sidewalk chalk. She hugs me for no good reason.

Beats Medicare.

ARNOLD ROSENFELD

I look at my grandchildren,
and now their children,
and I see how life continues.
While mine is running out,
theirs is just beginning.
The family will keep on going.
Circumstances change, and lifestyles change,
but family is family.
Baby hands and faces are the
same from generations on. Babies are life.
It's a wonder, all right.

DANIEL JOHNSON

Getting to know
the youngest people in my life
has been a joy.

FRANK TARLOFF

When I first received the news that I
was about to become a grandfather for
the seventh time, I knew I was in good company.
Arnold Palmer and Jack Nicklaus have more than
a dozen grandchildren between them.
You know something, when
these legendary pros readily admit
that they love these kids dearly,
and how family is so much more
important to them than the game of golf,
their claim to fame, it really puts life in perspective.
That's how all us Saturday hackers
should feel. Being a grandpa is
where it's at.
Grandkids are the heart makers and
the heart breakers.
Did you ever try to hug a golf trophy?

JACK SELLARS

*The power of our influence
upon our grandkids depends upon
the depth of our love for them.*

JON POWERS

*Nobody but a great-grandfather can
remember when people rested on Sunday
instead of Monday.*

BILL CRAIG

GRANDFATHER

The person in my life,
Who meant the most to me,
Was my loving grandfather,
Who saw me in a way
That no one else could see.
He understood the way I felt,
As if he had been there before,
He always had a hand to lend,
And a big loving heart with love to send.

He had followed the river of life,
As far as it would take him through,
But now the day had come for him too.
So many people who cared for him,
Wept in sorrow and turned very dim,
And the river began to flow again.
This river that was once my grandfather's
Had become my own that day.

ELLEN PRICE

THE FIRST WORDS TO THE GRANDFATHER

The young, bright-eyed man
looked at me
and said

"Get the electric trains ready
you're going to be a
grandfather!"

I wept with joyous tears
streaming down my face
holding both of their hands

I became locked in a threesome—whoops!—a
foursome
in the middle of the restaurant

Rushes of warm feelings of love flowed through
my body, warming me like the sun

I'm ready to be a good grandfather
a better grandfather than a father

I kissed the two lovers
and told them I loved them

I felt a tremendous shift
Our ancestors all in one movement
shifted with their approval and joy

I felt an ancestral cord tug
at us
"Live on—we love it"

The Clear One spoke
there has been a healing
I feel it twelve generations
back
Good work

You look beautiful together
Good work

MY GRANDPA—JOHN CRONE

My grandpa is a great guy
He just turned seventy-five
Even though he sleeps a lot
I'm sure glad he's alive.

My grandpa has lots of tools
He makes things out of wood
He is a mighty good craftsman
And people say he's good.

My grandpa likes to play cards
Like solitaire and poker
He thinks that he's a card shark
But I say he's a joker.

My grandpa likes to hunt and fish
He goes out with the guys
He always has a great time
And tells all sorts of lies.

I really love my grandpa
He is a lot of fun
Even though he sometimes yells
I think he's number one.

TRAVIS HEMENEZ, AGE TEN

Our children are here to stay,
but our babies and toddlers
and preschoolers are gone as fast
as they can grow up—and
we only have a short moment
with each. When you see a grandfather
take a baby in his arms,
you see that the moment
hasn't been long enough.

ST. CLAIR ADAMS SULLIVAN

My wise seventy-nine-year-old grandfather
made this toast to my dad at
his sixtieth birthday party:
"Here's to today, son, for you have
spent sixty years in preparation for
this moment; you will now begin to live.
At sixty, you have learned
what is really important.
You have overcome the worst forms of folly.
You have reached a 'balance' period of life,
knowing good from evil,
what is precious, what is worthless.
Peril is past, the mind is tranquil,
transgressions are forgiven,
affections are strong, envy is weak.
It is a reflective age,
when you feel contented
with a devoted wife,
loving children, loyal friendships,
and a bouncing grandchild on your knee."

SPENCER TRUMAN

When I get together at the clubhouse
after a round of golf with
my "old cronies,"
sharing stories about our grandchildren
is one of our favorite pastimes.
The one-upmanship that goes on
when comparing notes
is more amusing than any act
in a comedy club.

CALVIN MANNING

Never have children,
only grandchildren.

GORE VIDAL

PERMISSIONS ACKNOWLEDGMENTS

∷

Pp. 24–25: "Paul Tibbets IV proudly bears . . . legacy," by Paul Tibbets IV. Reprinted, with permission, from *The Columbus Dispatch.*

Pp. 41 (bottom), 49 (second from top), 94 (bottom), and 99: From *Milton Berle's Private Joke File,* by Milton Berle. Copyright © 1992 by Milton Berle. Used by permission of Crown Publishers Inc.

Pp. 42 (top) and 64 (second from top): From *Joke Soup,* by Judy Brown. Copyright © 1998 by Judy Brown. Used by permission of Universal Press Syndicate.

Pp. 46 (bottom) and 53 (second from bottom): From *Fatherhood,* by Bill Cosby. Copyright © 1986 by William H. Cosby, Jr. Used by permission of Doubleday, a division of Random House, Inc.

Pp. 60–61, 73 (top), and 80: "The Bowl of Milk," by Marie Hoy; "Gramps," by Juan Pablo Ardilo; "An Understanding Soul," by Heather Carollo. Reprinted with permission from *Skipping Stones* magazine, January–February 1997 (vol. 9, no. 1).

Pp. 75 (bottom), 77 (bottom), and 117 (top): From *100 Good Things That Happen as You Grow Older,* by Lauraine Snelling. Used by permission of Bristol Publishing Enterprises, Inc.

Pp. 106–8: "Gramps or Grandpa, the Role Is Really Just Grand," by Mike Harden. Reprinted, with permission, from *The Columbus Dispatch.*

Grateful acknowledgment to:

Pp. 21–22: Jennie Chin Hansen for permission to reprint "Remembering Grandfather Chin."

P. 26: Arthur Kornhaber.

Pp. 31–33: Gilad Evrony and The Third Generation Holocaust (web.wt.net/~gevro/) for permission to reprint "My Grandfather's Story."

Pp. 35 (top) and 89 (top): Mike Bellah and Our Best Years (www.bestyears.com) for permission to reprint "Five Famous Last Words for Midlifers" and an excerpt from *A Grandparent's Advice to Parents.*

P. 62: Chuck Nyren and Suite 101 (www.suite101.com) for permission to reprint "Grandma? Grandpa?"

P. 67: Arlene S. Uslander for permission to reprint "That's What Grandfathers Are For."

P. 70 (top): Ralph Reitenour for permission to reprint "The Happy Little Traveler."